T0113539

FROM DYSFUNCTIONAL TO FUNCTIONAL IN SEVENTEEN-DAYS

DORIS C. SMITH
EVANGELIST/KINGDOM LIFE COACH

authorHOUSE®

AuthorHouse™
1663 Liberty Drive
Bloomington, IN 47403
www.authorhouse.com
Phone: 833-262-8899

Published by AuthorHouse 09/08/2021

ISBN: 978-1-6655-3188-7 (sc)
ISBN: 978-1-6655-3198-6 (e)

Print information available on the last page.

From Dysfunctional to Functional In Seventeen-Days is a book for Men and Women. This book helps you to find answers to questions that you could possibly have about the will of God for your life.

It doesn't mean that you will have totally gotten everything "together" in seventeen-days, but you will have the "tools of Bibicial scriptures" you need to help do so.

This book will help you to heal from emotional and spiritual wounds. Also, from past hurts that you may have buried subconsciously.

There's Bibicial information through-out each Day that will help you move passed your hurts and get healed.

This book will show you how to build a relationship with the Lord. God desires relationship and not religion and this is the intent of this book. The book is kept simple and to the point.

ENJOY YOUR READING!

Dedication

SPECIAL THANKS
TO MY HEAVENLY FATHER
MY PARENTS
MR. OZELL & ORA BELL CONLEY
MY CHILDREN
LEVETTA CONLEY
(MISSISSIPPI REALTOR)
CHENITA (ANTONIO) BRYANT
MY GRANDCHILDREN
DEKETRICK DE'TERRION TODD
ANTHONY RANDELL WOODALL
MICHEAL DION WOODALL
ERICA LA'DAJAH BRYANT
ANTONIO DEON BRYANT JR.

Contents

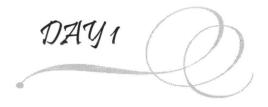

DAY 1

Dysfunctional Functioning

He who says they have "not" a dysfunctional family or at least a family member, let him now come to the alter and repent! We all have someone in the family where we say, "His elevator don't go all the way to the top floor!" or "She doesn't have all her marbles!" However, know that this is "not" the will of God.

What is Dysfunctional?

- Dysfunctional - NOT operating normally or properly. Or deviating from the norms of social behavior in a way regarded as bad.

An example would be: A man who was abused as a child, then grows up to become a mass murder, killing hundreds of boys and girls. We can look at this man and see that this is "not normal and it's regarded as bad." We would even say, "His elevator don't go all the way to the top floor, wouldn't we?

We look at this man but we never look at the "parents" of this man. Here's what we don't know about the man.

- What kind of parents he had?
- What "lack" of love or hate did he receive?
- Was he abused or kept in a cage?
- Was he molested or raped to cause such hostility?
- Did his parents do a lot of fighting before him?

So many things we don't know, while we're making judgement calls. You know the saying, "Before you judge a man, walk a mile in his moccasins!" This carries the meaning, "Don't find fault with the man that limps or stumbles along the road, unless you have worn the moccasins he wears." (Mary T. Lathrap)

A person growing up in a dysfunctional family have serious mental disorders. He may experience things such as verbal abuse, physical abuse, and emotional abuse. Most likely, there's a "lack" of emotional support. And, He's probably reared by a controlling parent, with little or no communication.

If you grew up in a family with mental disorders, you know that this can be hard. All of us can, at one time or another, remember something said that really "threw us off!" I can relate because there was a "lack" of verbal communication in "my" home. I mean, it was just certain things that we did not talk about. There were times that I "really" felt dysfunctional, and I had no one to discuss it with. Words were said that hurt and caused much "emotional dysfunction."

I was one of those "see more" children. I observed

everything. Nothing got past my eyes, when it came to dysfunction. Looking back now, I know it was a "trap" from the start. But any who!

I took everything to the "heart" literally. I had a Melancholy personality and it was "swinging like a pendulum" on a clock. I was a compulsive thinker. I couldn't seem to turn my mind off. I was sad one minute and confused the next. I used my humor to cover it up. We were a family that had much love and laughter, but we really didn't know how to express it in words.

I knew my parents loved me but it wasn't said "verbally" a lot. They didn't say, I don't love you but "not" saying it didn't help either. It's just as bad "in a child's mind!" This is why I tell my children every chance I get, "I love you." I know the effect of NOT saying it.

Ellen Perkins wrote, "Without doubt, the number one most psychologically damaging thing you can say to a child is, 'I don't love you' or 'you were a mistake." Can you imagine how that child feels or the thoughts that's going on in their mind?

Most times, in dysfunctional families, parents tend to be "too busy" with their own problems that they don't give their children what they are needing, which is love. Because of the "lack" of, children feel stressed and unwanted.

Some parents "may" want to do better but they don't know how. Their parents didn't do it, so because of the lack; it passes on to the next generation. Can we stop the madness?

Teaching has not been done as it should. Hosea 4:6 says, "My people are destroyed for "lack of knowledge." This is from both side: natural and spiritual. Charity "starts at home, then spread abroad." It is also time for the church (not all are doing this) to step up to the plate and start empowering the people of God so that they can fight a good fight of Faith. It has gone on long enough!

John 10:10 tells us, "The thief cometh not, but for to steal, and to kill, and to destroy: I am come that they might have life, and that they might have it more abundantly." When we think thief, we think Satan (even though he does), BUT... Jesus is talking about Leaders. The ones who are foolish gatekeepers that cannot tell the difference between a thief and a shepherd. Thieves who bring death, while Jesus is the one who brings "life."

God had a plan for the man in this example. The thief was the parents, who was supposed to teach the man... Even though the man's parents could have been the "same" way.

We must remember, we all have a "choice." Just like the son chose to "continue" with dysfunctional; the son could have chosen to "break" the dysfunctional pattern.

Stay with me as I teach in these Sessions.

Until tomorrow...

I pray Blessings upon you and that health and wealth become a part of your life.

Evangelist Doris C. Smith
KINGDOM LIFE COACH

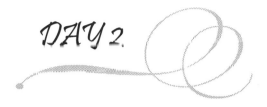

DAY 2.

God Has A Plan

This life can be hard. You have childhood struggles, pains, disappointments, heartaches, headaches and trials, but the Lord can make you stronger through all of these things. You must remember, they didn't come to break you, but to "make you."

Don't forget! Jeremiah 29:11, "For I know the plans I have for you," declares the Lord, "plans to give you hope and a future." (KJV) When you really get this, you will find that it takes on a deep meaning. It will be "powerful" once you apply it to "your" life.

As a Coach, I will help you to see the plan that God has for you. Now, it doesn't mean that you will not have hardships, or suffer BUT regardless, "IT" will work "for your good." So, never "stay" discouraged! You will work "through it" to prosper you and give you a hope and a future.

Kingdom Life Coaching is to help you identify your goals. It teaches you how to get a plan, so you can get the things God has for you. Now, the things I'm talking about is "not" cars, houses or land. I'm talking about "KINGDOM" things. Matthew 6:33 tells us, "But seek

FIRST 'His Kingdom' and 'His Righteousness', and all these things will be given to you as well." (NIV) This has always been, from the beginning, God's plan for your life. SEEK HIM!

Isn't it interesting that even in the Garden of Eden, seeking "things" ALWAYS brought destruction? Satan deceived Eve, then Eve persuaded Adam into "seeking for some "thing" they "already" had, which was the "knowledge" of good and evil. This caused the fall of man. Because Adam and Eve ate of the fruit, God sent them out of the Garden of Eden into the world. See, how he deceived them?

Satan uses "deception" to get a you to believe the "hypes and fantasies" that God is holding something back. He's still using that same tactic today. Genesis 2:15-17, "The Lord God took the man and put him in the Garden of Eden to work it and take care of it. And the Lord God "commanded" the man, "You are free to eat from any tree in the garden; but you "must not" eat from the tree of the knowledge of good and evil, for when you eat from "it" you will certainly die." (NIV)

God gave Adam and Eve a warning, specifically telling them, "They would die!" The obedience wasn't so much for "rules" but "relationship." The tree itself wasn't evil... BUT God had given instructions not to eat and Adam and Eve disobeyed. Adam listen to the voice of Eve's instead of obeying God.

God's plan is for you to prosper and grow spiritually "in" HIM. BUT...are you willing to do what it takes to bring it to pass? Are you willing to forget your plans for HIS PLANS?

Continue to stay with me as I talk about "IT."

Until next time...

I pray Blessings upon you and that health and wealth will become a part of your life!

Evangelist Doris C. Smith
KINGDOM LIFE COACH

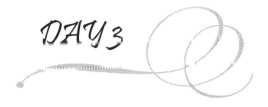

DAY 3

Know Who You Are

The first thing in seeking the Kingdom is "Knowing who you are." It is so important to know this because "when" you know this, you KNOW YOUR WORTH. Your worth is how you "value" yourself regardless, of what other people think or say about you. It's how you personally "see" yourself.

Growing up, I had no insight in knowing my value. Because of this, I had no idea how to reach my potentials. This is why God has called me to impart and share with you. It's amazing how our "mess" can be someone else's "message." He can take your "gloom" and turn it into your "GLORY." Praise God!

Examine your inner thoughts, watch your ways; they may have come from a "long line" of generational behaviors. Watch what you do, say, think and feel. An example would be, "Child, you know craziness runs in the family" or "My Mother had high blood pressure, so most likely, I'm going to have it as well." Watch what you say, even in goals that you want to accomplish! Don't do this! "Girl, you know I'm not smart enough to be a lawyer." or "I will always be broke!"

Don't speak negative thought over your life. Remember, Proverbs 18: 21 says, "Death and life is in the power of "your" tongue: and they that love it shall eat the fruit thereof." (KJV) Your words can speak death, or your words can speak life. You can build yourself up or you can tear yourself down. CHOOSE LIFE!

One thing that can help you is to know your "inborn personality." My personality type is Melancholy. Melancholic individuals tend to be analytical and detail-oriented. They are deep thinkers and feelers. They are introverted, which means they tend to hold a lot of feelings and emotions inside. You ask, "What's wrong?" and they will say, "Oh, nothing!" They like order, and are easily frustrated when it's out of order. They have lots of issues, yet they can be strong in their strength areas. Learn your strengths "and" your weaknesses. What you don't know "can hurt you." To know who you are, start by taking an online personality test. Remember, KNOWLEDGE IS THE KEY!

Psalms 139:13 tells us, "For you formed my innermost parts; You knit me [together] in my Mother's womb." There's a couple of words I want you to look at in this verse. One is "form" and the other one is "knit." Let's see what Google Dictionary says about these words.

- form - bring together parts or combine or create (something).
- knit - to make by interlocking loops of wool or other yarn with knitting needles or on a machine.

In that scripture, notice the Bible didn't say, you were "woven." He said, you were "knitted" in your Mother's womb.

Look at the DIFFERENCE!

Knit...
- Is made from ONE continuous fiber, like yarn or thread, which is repeats of loops to form a garment.

Woven...
- Unlike knits, woven materials contain MULTIPLE fibers, in form as a grid of rows and columns.

In the nine months, being in your Mother's womb, you became unique and with much treasure in you. You were intentional made and you were made exactly like HE wanted you!

Here's a passage from my book, "Facing Reality."

"Yes, the enemy started early trying to abort my calling. There were things that I struggled with as a child. Loneliness was my number one thing." Rejection was another. As you can see, I had "problems" and what I didn't know hurt me!

Children can have low self-esteem issues. This can cause many problems, IF they are not validated by their Fathers. Just as God validated Jesus, so must parents validate "their" children. In Matthew 3:17, "And suddenly a voice came from heaven saying, "This is My beloved Son, in whom I am well pleased. (NKJV).

In my childhood, I felt my Father did not love me or rather, he didn't "like" me. The enemy really magnified this thought in my head. Because of this, I struggled badly with low self-esteem, anxiety and depression. This brought on rejection.

The door for the Spirit of rejection to enter is most frequently opened during childhood, and even while a baby is still in its Mother's womb. When a child is unwanted, the fetus is opened for the entrance of a demon of rejection. I find that some persons are definitely repelled by such a suggestion. They think it's a terribly unfair that such a thing can be possible. We must remember the devil is no gentleman, and he is not regulated by rules of fair sportsmanship. Rather, he is extremely evil and does not hesitate for a moment to take full advantage of a situation which will foster his evil purposes. Satan delights in finding an Achilles heel for a target, choosing the weakest moments in life to attack. When is a person most defenseless? Before he is given birth and during infancy. (From the book, Pigs in a Parlor by, Frank & Ida Mae Hammond)

(This was my "IT") Note: You are in charge of your thoughts and being aware of what you're thinking helps you to come to true identity. Remember, this is what Satan wants to steal, "Your Identity."

The "Thief" comes "early in life" trying to destroy the plan of God. This is why it's IMPORTANT that parents and church leaders as well teach "Kingdom Building." Again, I say, "Teaching can either build up or tear down!"

In the next chapter, I will share with you how DYNAMIC God thinks you are. Continue to read and find out what's in you. Like Campbell Soup, "It's in There!"

Until next time...

I pray Blessings upon you and that health and wealth will become a part of your life!

Evangelist Doris C. Smith
KINGDOM LIFE COACH

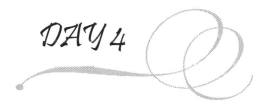

DAY 4

Making Adjustments

In order to get the full plan of God, you must be willing to "make adjustments." It's not like a "wish" list, thinking you can "wish it to come pass." Plans come through by just that...PLANNING. Like Campbell Soup, "It's in you and "you can do it." Remember, God thinks you are Dynamic!

What you want to do is, get Born again. Romans 10:9 tells us, "If you "declare" with your mouth, Jesus is Lord, and "believe" in your heart that God raised Him from the dead, you will be saved."

- Declare - To say something in a solemn and emphatic manner. To proclaim.

God "expects" you to make adjustments, once you get saved. When God spoke to Moses, he was challenged to make some big adjustments. He was told to leave the place, where he lived for forty-years. Hebrew 11:27 says, "By faith he forsook Egypt, not fearing the wrath of the King: for he endured, as seeing him who is invisible." (KJV)

I have the ABC magnets on my refrigerator and it reads, "HE IS LORD!" That means, "In my house, if God says it's wrong, then "that settles it!". He leads, I follow! I, (1) Confessed, (2) made Him Savior, (3) then Lord. That's the bottom Line!

Now, this didn't happen over-night and it wasn't always easy. I had to make many adjustments. Even though it wasn't easy, I can say, "It has been worth it!" You will find it's worth it, as well.

- Adjustments means - a small alteration or movement made to achieve a desired fit, appearance, or result. Or it can mean, the process of adapting or becoming used to a "new" situation.

See, once you accept Jesus as Savior, the next step would be for you to "make HIM Lord! Now, this change the game as to who's in charge. You no longer make decisions as to what "you want, you think, or believe." Jesus now governs your life.

Some adjustments may cause change in friendships, relationships, or even your job. There will be some easy adjustments but, some may be hard. The harder ones will require faith. This will probably be "totally" different than what you are used to doing. However, it is "necessary!"

Adjustments brings about a change, and as Dr. Creflo Dollar says, "Change ain't change until you change!" Changing you, change others. You must understand that it's not "just" about you. Others salvation "hang in the basket" of you getting saved.

Many times, I wanted to give up BUT... I thought of my Children and Grand-children. That's what started me... BUT NOW, I think about how Jesus went on the cross and died that I might have Eternal Life NOW...That's what keeps me. Praise God!

"I'm saved and I'm loving it! I don't mean like McDonald's!!!

Until next time...

I pray Blessings upon you and that health and wealth will become a part of your life!

Evangelist Doris C. Smith
KINGDOM LIFE COACH

Day 5

Going Slow But Steady

The Woman at the Well is a great example. We don't know her name or age, BUT...her conversation with the Lord is one of His longest one-on-one chats recorded. This is reason enough to give our Sister from Samaria a fresh look.

Picture This!

It was around noon, on a very hot day; Jesus being tired from traveling, chose a sensible rest stop, which was Jacob's well. Jacob's well was outside the town of Sychar.

This unnamed woman came by, she had a clay jar in her hand. Jesus made a simple request of her, "Will you give me a drink?" She gave three reasons why she couldn't,

- Jews weren't supposed to speak to Samaritans,
- Men weren't permitted to address women without their husbands present, and
- Rabbis had no business speaking to "shady" women.

Jesus was willing to throw out the rules, but our Woman at the Well wasn't. She reminded Him, "You're a Jew and I am a Samaritan Woman." She asked, "How can You ask me for a drink?" She was focusing on the Law; while Jesus focused on Grace.

He stated to her, "If you only knew the Gift of God; Especially, the Gift that came by the Grace of the one man, Jesus Christ!" Instead of insisting she pour Him a drink, the Lord offered her, Living Water. Water from the ground was common, but "Living water!"

Now, He had her attention. The Woman at the well pointed out the obvious. "You have nothing to draw with and the well is deep. "Where can you get this Living water? Her curiosity prompted her to ask questions, as seekers do today. But, Jesus knew too well, how to handle doubt and disbelief.

To quench her Spiritual thirst, the Lord first confessed the truth about plain water. "Everyone who drinks that water will be thirsty again." Then Jesus made a bold promise. BUT... "Whoever drinks the water I give him, will never thirst." In one sentence, He shifted from everyday life to "Everlasting Life."

Was our girl ready for that leap of Faith? No Ma'am, No Sir! She wanted whatever He was offering, but only so she could avoid going back to the well. If we're honest, we get this same way. Eager to satisfy our physical desires, we override our Spiritual needs.

Jesus told her, "Go get your husband and come back!" This was not a strange request, since women couldn't talk alone with a man in a public place. Jesus' request was more about uncovering truth that about following society's rules.

She confessed, "I have no husband!"...Jesus affirmed her answer, then "gently" exposed her sin. "The fact is, you have had five husbands, and the man you now have is not your husband." (IT'S NACHOS!)

Five marriages weren't what was making her a sinner. Sharing her bed with the sixth man, who wasn't her husband was the sin.

But, did she confess? No, she most certainly did "not!" She changed the subject. She talked about

- Worship,
- Jerusalem, and
- The difference between Jews and Samaritans.

Due to warfare, famine, disease, and injury; men in those days dropped like dead flies. A widow became...

- A beggar,
- Prostitute,
- Or another man's wife.

The Woman at the Well did her best to shut down the conversation with Jesus. "When the Messiah comes, He will explain everything to us." How shocked she must have been at Jesus' revelation. "I who speak to you am He!" The next moment, the arrival of His Followers confirmed His identity and gave the Woman time to process the Truth.

The Anointed One had come! Over-joyed, she left her water jar and went back into town to urge her neighbors, "Come, see a Man who told me everything I ever did."

Notice how Jesus took His time and used Wisdom in ministering to the Woman. Most people don't "hang in there" because they start out too fast. Just a Jesus slowly ministered to the Woman at the Well, so must we, as Leaders. He gave her time to process the Truth.

You must FIRST "CATCH THE FISH" BEFORE YOU CAN "CLEAN IT." Some Leaders have "cooked" the fish (person) and the "guts" are still in them. Some have been cooked and they still have "scales" on them. What's the hurry?

Give them time! Teach them what they just received. Tell them all the FINE-PRINT. Salvation comes with a price and you must be willing to pay it. You can refuse because it is a FREE-WILL.

IF we minister it like Jesus did with the Woman at the Well, Christian will be stable. Take them slow, so they can get an understanding. Proverbs 4:4 tells us, "Wisdom is the PRINCIPAL THING, therefore get wisdom: and with all thy getting get understanding. (KJV)

You may not "get it" as fast as the next person or slow as another, BUT...the main thing is that you "get it." Always get an understanding of what is being taught. Hold fast to what you "know!" God will confirm in your Spirit HIS TRUTH. TRUST HIM!

Until next time...

I pray Blessings upon you and that health and wealth will become a part of your life!

Evangelist Doris C. Smith
KINGDOM LIFE COACH

DAY 6

Denounce The Spirit Of Pride

The Biblical sin of pride refers to "Having a high mind." You think this is good BUT... it actually comes from poor self-worth and shame. You in reality, feel badly about yourself, but try to make yourself feel superior in the public. You look at others flaws and hide your own. You love criticizing others and you praise yourself.

You are looking at yourself in "tinted" glasses, and using a magnifying glass while looking at others. This is pride and wrong! You have to denounce that your way is "wrong" and "GOD'S WAY IS RIGHT!"

- Denounce - Publicly declare to be wrong or evil.
- Pride - A feeling of deep pleasure or satisfaction derived from one's "own" achievements. Also, when you think you're better than someone else.

I had the "next door neighbor" to Pride. The Spirit I had to was "Unknowingly Vows, which derived from Pride." I made them concerning my Father. My Dad had a Choleric temperament. He was a man that, "What He says, goes!" He most definitely "Ruled the nest!" He was very bossy, and impatient. I thought, He was the meanest man I knew. I couldn't wait to leave home.

So, I made vows of what life would be for me, when I "get out." I made vows as to what I would tolerate and NOT tolerate. I didn't realize I wasn't the one in charge of my life. And little did I know, the danger in making those vows.

I realize today, that those childhood vows actually affected my adult life and marriage life. Anytime I heard my Father's voice, in my marriages, I went back to that "little girl" back home. I would react, in thought, the same way, "I got to get out of here!" My saying was, "I wouldn't put up with that as long as Job stayed in the army." It was a saying that I heard my Mother say, when it came to "tolerating stupid stuff." I'm saying what she's saying, "not knowing "Job" or "even how long" he stayed in the army!" Making those vows was one of the worst things I could have ever done.

If you have done this, I beg of you to denounce them now, in the Name of Jesus! You are not in charge of your life. You did not make yourself. When you make vows, you are saying, "I" "I" "I."

"I" is not in charge, JESUS IS! Too often we make vows rashly. We make them in the midst of an emotional moment. We give no thoughts to what it takes to fulfill that vow.

Vows should "never" be made lightly, emotionally, or quickly. Proverb 20:25 tells us, "It's dangerous to promise something to God too quickly." "After you've thought about it, it may be too late."

"Watch your mouth!" Old folks often said this and this still hold as good advice today. I had to denounce those vows because, I realize the consequences that they had caused me, in my life and marriages. Pride caused me to feel, I didn't need my Daddy. I could handle my "own" life, I thought. I didn't know, to stop and acknowledge God for directions. See, The "lack" of knowledge?

Pride causes you to feel that YOU don't need God to accomplish what you want. Oh, how sadly wrong you are! YOU WILL NEVER WALK IN WHAT HE HAS FOR YOUR LIFE WITHOUT HIM.

God is your Creator. And just like everything you buy comes with a manual, the Bible is yours and you must learn to walk according to His word. I encourage you to, if you haven't already, to drop your pride, denounce any unknowingly vows that you may have made. If you are not sure, pray and ask God to reveal it to you.

Until tomorrow...

I pray Blessings upon you and that health and wealth will become a part of your life.

Evangelist Doris C. Smith
KINGDOM LIFE COACH

Day 7

Hear The Word Of God

Now that you have confessed Jesus as Lord and you have denounced your pride; get some word! I don't mean RELIGION because, Religion is only a duty! I am talking about "WORD." God's word, God's Promises!

Romans 10:14 says, "How then shall they call on Him in whom they have not believed? And how shall they believe in Him of whom they have not heard? And how shall they hear without a preacher?"

Three questions are asked here.

- How then shall they call on Him in whom they have not believed?
- How shall they believe in Him of whom they have not heard?
- How shall they hear without a Preacher?

This shows you how important God wants you to get the word. I have nothing against preaching, but; I'm a preacher that promotes Teaching. Preaching expounds on the word that has "already" been taught. If you don't know the word, then preaching is only "hollering at you."

It's like discipling your child. If you have not taught him right from wrong, then whipping him serves no purpose. He doesn't know "why" and all he thinks is, "I have mean parents and because they constantly whip me, they must not love me!"

Hearing the word is not just "knowing how to quote it backward and forward", it's applying it in your everyday life. You must do what God word says, standing strong in faith, and not wavering.

I was blessed to get into some awesome classes that really helped me. They taught callings, purpose, gifts, how to pray and what to pray for. They also taught, how to know your calling, which was something I really needed an answer to. I praise God for every class today.

Hearing instructions for your life is important. Whether on the job, school, or in your Ministry. Why? Because before you can do a job, or follow instruction, you "first" must be told what it is that you're to do.

If you go to the store, to get some things that I sent you to get and you forgot to get the list, how will you bring back what I asked for? You can't! Even though, you had good intentions, you still can't get the job done. Or, if you took the list, went to the store and you can't read; You still can't carry out instructions.

The Eunuch did not fully understand what he was reading and "desired" Phillip that he would sit with him and "explain" the scripture to him. Phillip taught the Eunuch, and the Eunuch heard and obeyed the Gospel. (Acts 8:26-39) When you "know" what to do, the job will not be hard at all.

Continue to stay with me

I pray Blessings upon you this day and that health and wealth will become a part of your life!

Evangelist Doris C. Smith
KINGDOM LIFE COACH

Day 8

Be A Doer Of The Word

James 1:22-25, "But be doers of the word, and not hearers only, deceiving your own selves. For if any be a hearer of the word, and not a doer, he is like unto a man beholding his natural face in a glass: For he beholdeth himself, and goeth his way, and straightway forgetteth what manner of man he was."

God desires that we listen to hear, and hear to apply. Doing otherwise, is worthless! It's like applying make-up to your face, then, you wash it off and ask, "Don't my make-up look pretty?" How would we know? You have to put the make-up on and let it stay. Otherwise, you have "no evidence" of the make-up on your face. Evidence says, "You done the work!" Evidence shows proof!

- Doer - A person who ACTS rather than merely talking or thinking.

The Doer "acts and apply" the word to his "daily life." You should be a doer as well. You must "act and apply" the word "in" your life. Putting the word to work will change your life. Changing brings on "transformation." Remember,

I quoted Dr. Creflo Dollar, "Change ain't change until you change!" Change is referring to your "mind-set." His word will "re-new" our mind, causing you to become more like Him (Jesus) every day.

How important is it to be a doer of God's word? Doing otherwise is like "fool's gold!" Fool's gold is any flashy but ultimately worthless investment.

After preaching a sermon on the Mount, Jesus said, we should be doers of the word. If not, it's like looking in the mirror and forgetting what you look like. James 1:23-24, "For if anyone is a hearer of the word and not a doer, he is like a man who looks at his natural face in the mirror; For once he has looked at himself and gone away, he has immediately forgotten what kind of person he was." If your attitude or character doesn't change, you will always be the same. You are robbing yourself from the blessings of God.

You seem to have it together on the outside but in reality, you are still walking in the old man. From my book, Facing Reality, "Think about the things that may have you hindered in life. Don't be afraid, shame or even in denial."

If you see flaws, fix them by using the Word of God. Allow the word to be your mirror. Just as you would apply the make-up, so would you apply the word. If you're a man... if you had a flat tire on your car, surely, you wouldn't take off the flat tire and put it back on. No, you would change the flat tire to put on the tire that has air in it.

When the word shows you sin, repent and stop doing it! When it chastises you, correct yourself! No one has to tell you when you are doing wrong. Even a baby, at a certain age, knows when he's doing something wrong. The word is your "measuring stick" for you to use, in examining yourself. However, you must be willing to do it "truthfully." Otherwise, you're deceiving yourself.

Allow the word of God to bring you to the new person. Start decreeing that the "old man is dead and the new man now lives in you!" You can do this...

Until tomorrow...

I pray Blessing on you this day and that health and wealth will become a part of your life!

Evangelist Doris C. Smith
KINGDOM LIFE COACH

Day 9

The Truth

The Blessings comes by knowing Truth. John 8:32 tells us, "THEN you will know the truth, and the truth will set you free." What truth will set you free? The truth that you KNOW.

Then, what is truth?

• Truth - is in fact a verified or indisputable fact.

"Jesus is the Son of God. He is the way, the truth and the life. That's Truth! John 14:6. (KJV)

If it's not truth then it's falsehood. "We" as a people have been taught "more" things that had NOTHING to do with truth. Some of these false truths was, turning around when a black cat's crossing the road; throwing salt over your back for good luck; when the broom hits your feet, spit on the broom; or splitting a pole was bad luck.

And what about the church, not being able to play marble because the Bible says, "marble not!" The word was "marvel", not marble. Or when they would say, "touch not the unclean things and wouldn't touch ash trays because they had cigarettes butts in them." Help Lord!

Do you see how not knowing truth can keep you bound?

God does not want you bound up. That's why he came to set the captives free. You have lived in bondage long enough. It's time to get the truth and allow that truth to set you free!

Freedom is what God wants for you. John 8:36 tells us, "IF the Son therefore shall make you free, ye shall be free indeed." You have been set free from sin and have become "slaves to righteousness."

The Bible talks a lot about Truth. The things that are true can be proven. How can you prove your "true" freedom, from "false" belief? By saying what the word of God says! An example would be, having constant migraine headaches. "Truth" is, "But He was wounded for "your" transgression, He was bruise for "your" inequities: the chastisement of "your" peace was upon Him; and with His stripes "you" are healed. Isaiah 53: 5:8 (KJV)

So, "you" take truth and apply it to that migraine headache and decree "your" healing. Remember, God wants you well. If you really want to learn how-to walk-in truth, practice the skills. What does this mean? Line up your "beliefs and behavior" according to the word of God. Just like you believe in all those "superstitions", believe the Word of God the same way. Where will this take you? To having a transformed mind. Before you know it, your practice will have become a "Way of Life."

Until tomorrow...

I pray Blessings on you this day and that health and wealth becomes a part of your life!

Evangelist Doris C. Smith
KINGDOM LIFE COACH

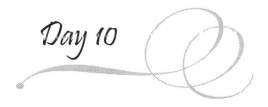

Day 10

The Righteousness Of God

There is YOUR RIGHT and GOD'S RIGHT. So, Who's right? Well, you already know the answer to that! What is right and how does it relate to RIGHTEOUSNESS?

- Right- True or correct as a fact.
- Righteousness - Free from guilt or sin.

You are not righteous in God's eyes because "you are so good" or "because of your good works" but because of what Jesus did on the Cross. This is why He came and died for you, because HE KNEW you needed a Savior. All of "our" righteousness was as a "filthy" rag.

"Not by works of righteousness which "we" have done, but according to His mercy HE SAVED US, by the washing of regeneration, and renewing of the Holy Spirit, which He shed on us abundantly through Jesus Christ our Savior." Titus 3:5-6 (KJV)

Ephesians 1:4 tells us, "For HE CHOSE US in Him BEFORE the creation of the world to be Holy and blameless in His sight. In love." (NIV) So, when you think you are a

Mr. or Ms./Mrs. Goody Two-Shoe, think again because "it's not your" righteousness. (It's Nachos!)

The Holy Spirit was sent down by the Father upon Jesus as a dove in His Baptism. "Jesus, when He was Baptized, went up straightway out of the water; and lo, the heavens were opened unto Him, and He saw the Spirit of God descending like a dove, and lighting upon Him. (Matthew 3:16)

The Holy Spirit equipped Him for the purpose of Ministry. The Holy Spirit was the key in Jesus accomplishing His destiny and this same key is necessary for you in accomplishing your purpose.

You are unique to God. He has chosen you to do a special mission in this life. I can't do yours and you can't do mine.

These Sessions comes daily to encourage you, if you haven't already started, ask God what is "your mission" and start doing it.

Tune in tomorrow...

I pray Blessings upon you this day and that health and wealth will become a part of your life!

Evangelist Doris C. Smith
KINGDOM LIFE COACH

Day 11

We All Come Short Of The Glory!

None of us is perfect! We all lack something in one area or another. But, Thank God for His Grace and Mercy!

Moses was a Murder, King Saul tried to kill King David, and Peter denied Jesus. David had Uriah killed to take his wife, Bathsheba.

David and Bathsheba are one of the most told accounts in the Bible. King David, while walking on his rooftop, spotted Bathsheba while she was bathing. David inquired about her, by asking his servant "who was she?" The servant told him that she was Uriah the Hittite wife. Uriah was one of the mighty men in David's (himself) army.

However, that didn't stop David. He summoned Bathsheba to his Palace and slept with her. She later found out she was pregnant and told David. David tried to hide his sin by first sending for Uriah and tricking him to sleep with Bathsheba. When that didn't work, he set it up for Uriah to be killed in battle.

Bathsheba mourned for a while but soon married David and gave birth to a son. The son died. The thing David done displeased the Lord. 2 Samuel 11:27 reads, "And when the mourning was past, David sent and fetched her to his house, and she became his wife, and bare him a son. But the thing that David had done displeased the Lord." (KJV)

He repented and God still used not only him but the other mentioned names as well. That's because in spite of our short-comings God can, when we "honestly" repent, still use us for His Glory.

Repentance for sin and serving God go hand in hand. You cannot repent for sin unless you have a servant-heart. And you can't serve, unless you repent of your sins. David prayed, "Hide your face from my sins, and blot out all of my iniquities." (Psalms 51:9) You must become Godly sorrow. Not just because you got caught!

David act with Bathsheba was no accident, and he could not excuse it in any kind of way. This is what we have to do, IF we sin. We have to "call a spade a spade!" We fell short, we missed the mark, then we say as David said, in Psalms 51:10, "Create in me a clean heart, O God; and renew a right spirit within me." (KJV)

David said it was against thee and thee only have I sin. David repented with a broken spirit; a broken and contrite heart.

- Broken - Having been fractured or damaged and no longer in one piece. Smashed or shattered.
- Contrite - Feeling or expressing remorse or affected by guilt.

When you truly love God, it does bring a feeling of remorse, knowing that you have done a thing that was displeasing in His sight. However, we thank God that He is a God of a first, second, third, fourth and many more chances.

The thing to REMEMBER, YOU MUST GET IT RIGHT WITH GOD. DO NOT ASSUME because you still go to Church that it is well. It might be well with you, but is it well with God?

Until tomorrow...

I pray Blessings upon you this day and that health and wealth become a part of your life!

Evangelist Doris C. Smith
KINGDOM LIFE COACH

Day 12

The Real Church Is "In You"

For many, Church is traditional. It's just what we've learned to do each Sunday. For most, it's like as Joyce Meyers could say, "This is the way we go to Church, go to Church, go to Church, this is the way we go to Church, Every Sunday Morning.

Jesus died for the Church, however; the Church isn't the building. THE CHURCH IS YOU! You are the Church, not the four walls that you sit in each Sunday. When you leave Church, the building is still there and standing. You take the Church with you. Everywhere you go, the Church goes too.

Religion has told Christians, for so long, that the Church was the building, and we now believe it. Now, we have a bunch of buildings that no one is attending and "no relationships" with the Lord Jesus. How sad! Relationship has always been Jesus desire.

HE DIED TO HAVE A RELATIONSHIP WITH YOU.

You would think the Pandemic would have drawn "us" closer but it seemed as if it has caused us to do "more" Church.

- Relationship - The way in which two people are connected.

GET IN A RELATIONSHIP WITH GOD YOURSELF AND DON'T BE SHAKEN IN YOUR MIND. FALL IN LOVE WITH GOD MORE THAN YOUR DO THE WORLD!

There is NO RELATIONSHIP in your life more important than the one you have with your Creator. Spending time with God and listening to Him help deepen your relationship. If you feel you have nothing to talk about, just listen to Him.

When you are not sure what to pray, pray the scriptures. Psalms 23 is a good one. "The Lord is my Shepherd; I shall not want. He maketh me to lie down in green pastures." (KJV)

Being real with God is important. He knows where you are in Him and "where you "are not." Pastor Maria Gardner said that her Grandmother told her these words, on her death bed, "Baby, IF you be real, God will use you!" The same applies to you, IF you be real.

"Faking it just to make it" will no longer work. Who wants to fake Church all their life and stand before God in judgement and He say, "Depart from me, you who work inequity." (Matthew 7:23)

Strive to enter in a relationship with God. Day by day, step by step. This doesn't happen overnight but with time, trust and truth; it will happen. I have found nothing better than my relationship with God. Neither will you!

Continue to stay with me...

I pray Blessings upon you this day and that health and wealth become a part of your life.

Evangelist Doris C. Smith
KINGDOM LIFE COACH

Day 13

The Blood Covenant

To keep it simple, the Blood Covenant is a promise made by God that He will choose a people for Himself and bless them. This Covenant establishes a close bond between two people, not necessarily linked by kinship, but still desire relationship.

You know how some say, "We are Brothers but not by the same Mother." They are referring to the "closeness and bond" they have. Even though, they are not "blood kin" they are "bond kin."

If you lost blood for any reason, in most cases, the doctors would find another person with your type and put it into your body, so you can live. With this in mind, we can clearly see that blood is important. And not just "any blood" will do!

- Covenant - A binding agreement made by two or more parties. A contract or a promise.

The Covenant was God's idea. Man was unable to keep the Covenant so God, because He loved us so, made it possible by sacrificing the Blood of Jesus.

Jesus left Heaven and came into this world to be nothing less than the FINAL SACRIFICE for every sin. This put a permanent end to the need for any more "Blood Sacrificial."

"JESUS PAID IT ALL!

Matthew 26:28 Jesus said, "For this is My blood of the New Covenant, which is shed for "many" for the remission of sins."

John 1:29 also tells us, the next day John saw Jesus coming toward him, and said, "Behold! The Lamb of God who takes away the sin of the world!"

WHAT A MIGHTY GOD WE SERVE!

A Covenant with God is important and vital (necessary) to Him. It is NOT to be taken lightly. Life is in the blood, so is our life with Jesus!

Tune in tomorrow as we continue...

I pray Blessings upon you this day and that health and wealth become a part of your life.

Evangelist Doris C. Smith
KINGDOM LIFE COACH

Day 14

The Mind Of Christ

Growing up, this was a very popular slogan, "A mind is a terrible thing to waste." Even today, ads still warn against "wasting your mind." What the mind is, "The mind is a beautiful thing!"

The Bible speak a lot about the mind. I will share a few scriptures.

Matthew 22:37
* "Thou wilt keep him in perfect peace, whose mind is stayed on thee: because he trusted in thee." (KJV)

Philippians 4:7
* "And the peace of God, which passeth all understanding, shall keep your hearts and your minds through Christ Jesus." (KJV)

Romans 12:2
* "And be not conformed to this world: but be ye transformed by the renewing of your mind, that ye may prove what is that good, and acceptable, and perfect, will of God." (KJV)

Living a life for Christ is impossible to do until you get the mind of Christ. Changing your mind was Jesus's main Sermons. He often challenged the people to change "their thinking" and get the mind of Christ. If your mind doesn't change, you will only add "your thoughts" on the words you read.

Staying in your old mind keeps you in your old ways. It will only allow you to do things "in the outer man." That's what you call doing it for an "outside show." It's all flesh!

But when you get the mind of Christ, then it becomes a way of life. Philippians 2:5 tells us, "Let this mind be IN YOU, which was also IN CHRIST JESUS." It didn't say, "Let it be outside you." YOU MUST HAVE THE SAME MIND-SET THAT JESUS HAVE! How can two walk together, except they agreed?

It takes Spiritual maturity to have the mind of Christ. As I talked about earlier, You must RECIEVE JESUS AS LORD AND SAVIOR. This is a daily thing. Just as you take your medicines daily, so do you have to talk, read, and grow in the word.

IT IS NECCESSARY!

Just as your mind was once program to the world ways, so does it have to be programmed to the ways of God. Trying to do them both, causes you to become spiritual schizophrenia.

- Schizophrenia - is a serious mental disorder in which people interpret reality abnormally. Schizophrenia may result in some combination of hallucinations, delusions, and extremely disordered thinking, and behavior that impairs daily functioning, and can be disabling

- Delusions - False beliefs not based in reality.
- Hallucinations - Seeing or hearing things that don't exist.

Examples of spiritual disorders:

- Saved without confessing Christ. (spiritual delusion)
- Hearing God promise you Blessings when you are out of HIS will. (spiritual schizophrenia)
- You see God blessing you with money and you spend it as fast as you get your hands on it. (spiritual hallucination)

God promises always comes with "IF" and "THEN." These Blessings may APPEAR TO BE FROM GOD but they are not. When it comes to the Blessings of God and His promises, there are conditions put upon them. In Deuteronomy 28 it tells of the Blessings of Obedience and Disobedience.

Stay with me as we continue to learn...

I pray Blessings upon you this day and that health and wealth become a part of your life.

Evangelist Doris C. Smith
KINGDOM LIFE COACH

Day 15

Pour Into Yourself

Sometimes, you're so busy trying to help others; you forget yourself. You sometimes do as the Indian who, knew there were ten who went fishing, but in his count; he only counted nine. After counting many times, it dawns on him that he forgot to "count himself."

You pour into others the over-flow, not what's God gave "You. "Oh boy, Did I have to learn this lesson, and still have to "constantly" remind myself even to this day.

When you don't care for you first, you can look for "burn-out" to come. Spiritual burn-out is when you take on too much spiritual work and you don't allow "your" spirit to rest.

* Burn-out - is generally considered a state of physical or emotional exhaustion from ongoing stress.

You will start feeling tired and exhausted. You start having lack of entergy and strength. There were days I could have stayed in the bed "all" day. You seem to be sluggish and drained. You have to "make" yourself push forward.

Beware of these signs. Learn how to say, "Not Today!" It's not a curse word.

Take time for yourself. Refresh yourself in Worship Music. Sometimes, I just play it through-out my house. Get the atmosphere changed, so that the presence of the Lord can come in. Ask the Lord to lead and guide you to the people who you need to talk too. There are some people who can just drain your entergy. When it's like that, let your answer machine get it and call them back at a better time for you.

Burn-out makes you feel weary. We know that this feeling does not come from God. In Matthew 11:28-30, it tells us, "Come unto me, all ye that labour and are heavy laden, and I will give you rest. Take my yoke upon you, and learn of me; for I am meek and lowly in heart: and ye shall find rest unto your souls. For my yoke is easy, and my burden is light." (KJV)

Serving in ministry can be exhausting. Any position where you "give out" can be tiresome. Jobs like, Pastor, Counselor, Ministry of Deliverance, Life Coach or any of the Five-Fold Ministry. You can get exhausted in other jobs like, Teacher, Parent, Caregiver, or any one in the School System. Daily living in the hustle and bustle is tiresome. The Pandemic did not help matters!

There's a lot of emotions associated with burn-out. But here's a tip to help: Mind your "own" business. If we mind our own business, we can stay busy all day. Life is much easier when you mind your own business. Everything is NOT for you to fix. Some people want fix their problems because they know "you" will.

There comes a time when you have to say, "Not my

monkeys, not my circus!" Meaning, don't drag me into your drama and your issues. I am not getting involved.

Until tomorrow...

I pray Blessings upon you this day and that health and wealth become a part of your life.

Evangelist C. Smith
KINGDOM LIFE COACH

Day 16

The Importance Of Rest

When you're not feeling your best, it's hard to stay focus or study as you should. That's why IT'S IMPORTANT that you take good care of yourself. As I stated on yesterday, "POUR INTO YOURSELF!" Sometimes, "we" take care of others and our health go lacking.

LET'S STOP IT!!!

Get you some rest, take a vacation or va-cate from people every now and then. Remember, your body is the temple where the Holy Spirit lives. Do you not know your temple needs rest? 1 Corinthians 6:19 tells us, "What? Know ye not that your body is the temple of the Holy Ghost which is in you, which ye have of God, and ye are not your own?" (KJV)

Jesus often went to be along from the disciples, especially; when He prayed. Mark 1:35 tells us, "Now in the morning, having risen a long while before daylight, He went out and departed to a SOLITARY PLACE; AND THERE HE PRAYED (ALONE).

Luke 6:12, "One of those days Jesus went out to a mountainside to pray, and spent the night praying to God."

(ALONE) When you're dealing with people all the time, it's tiresome. Honey! sometimes, you have to get away.

Rest is NECCESSARY! A lack of it causes problems with your concentration and memory. It can affect your immune system, cause stress, and cause you to have bad mood swings.

Learn to set boundaries when it comes to your rest. You don't have to be "everything to everybody." If you get sick, who will take care of you? Will any of the people that have been calling you be there? Maybe or Maybe NOT!

Everyone' pulls on you, thinking you have all the answers, BUT WHERE DO THE YOU GO WHEN YOU NEED SOMEONE TO PULL ON?

Your body can naturally heal itself but you have to give it what it NEEDS in order to do so. And sometimes, it's a simple thing called R-E-S-T. Try it, you're like it!!!

Get you some today...

I pray Blessings upon you this day and that health and wealth will become a part of your life.

Evangelist Doris C. Smith
KINGDOM LIFE COACH

Day 17

How To Know God's Will

Read the Word of God
- Proverb 3:5-6 tells us, "Trust in the Lord with all thine heart; and lean not unto thine own understanding. In all thy ways acknowledge Him, and He shall direct thy paths. (KJV)

Pray & Listen
- 1 John 5:14-15 tells us, "And this is the confidence that we have in Him, that, if we ask any thing according to His will, He heareth us: And if we know that He hear us, whatsoever we ask, we know the petitions that we desired of Him." (KJV)

Listen to Godly Counsel
- Proverb 19:20-21 tells us, "Hear counsel, and receive instruction, that thou mayest be wise in thy latter end. There are many devices in a man's heart; nevertheless, the counsel of the Lord, that shall stand." (KJV)

Be Watchful of a Restless Spirit
- Hebrews 4:12 tells us, "For the Word of God is quick, and powerful, and sharper than any two-edged sword, piercing even to the dividing asunder of soul and spirit, and of the joints and marrow, and is a discerner of the thoughts and intents of the heart." (KJV)

Walk in Faith
- Hebrews 11:6 tells us, "But without faith it is impossible to please Him: for He that cometh to God must believe that He is, and that He is a rewarder of them that diligently seek Him. (KJV)

It is time to open up to what the Lord has for YOU! As a Life Coach I will help you identify your purpose. On the following pages, there are questions and scriptures to help. It is important that you are honest in your answers. It may take some time and meditating.

I pray this booklet have help you and I pray it was a blessing to you. Until next time!

Evangelist Doris C. Smith
KINGDOM LIFE COACH

Kingdom Life Coaching
Evangelist Doris C. Smith

Put Simply, Kingdom Life Coaching is a process that aims to improve your performance and help you to get to your "here and now."

Kingdom Life Coaching equips and empower you to put first the Kingdom of God wherever you go.

Kingdom Life Coaching Helps YOU:

1. Identify Your Goals
2. Get a Clear Plan of Action
3. Achieve What You Want Quicker

The Kingdom Life Coach is there to help the Coachee achieve the specific, whether personal or professional goals by teaching, guiding and training.

If you commit to the study in this booklet, success is sure to come. I do not believe it takes years of doing this, it only takes you to total surrender and commit to God.

I pray God's blessings as you leap into your New Way of Life. If you need further help, please don't hesitate. You can reach me three ways:

1. 1. E-mail me: dorissmith217@yahoo.com
2. You can call me: 662-614-3402
3. You can write: P.O. Box 174; Grenada, Ms. 38901

Everybody wants to be successful. Life is designed for you to succeed. God is committed to your success. It is built into creation.

God's blessings as you go forward!

Evangelist Doris C. Smith
Kingdom Life Coach

Getting Started

There are five (5) questions you want to ask yourself. I will give them to you, with scriptures to meditate on.

- 1. How would you identify yourself?

2 Corinthians 5:21: "God made Him (Jesus) who had no sin to be sin for us, so that in Him we might become the righteousness of God."

Galatians 4:7: "Therefore you are no longer a slave but a son, and if a son, then an heir of God through Christ."

- 2. Where are you from?

Psalms 139:13: "For you formed my inward parts; You wove me in my Mother's womb."

1 Peter 1:23: "I am chosen by God who called me out of the darkness of sin and into the light and life of Christ so I can proclaim the excellence and greatness of who He is."

- 3. Why are you here?

Genesis 1:28: "And God blessed them, and God said unto them. Be fruitful, and multiply, and replenish the earth, and subdue it: and have dominion over the fish of the sea, over the fowl of the air, and over every living thing that moveth upon the earth"

1 Corinthians 6:20: "For ye are bought with a price: therefore, glorify God in your body, and in your spirit, which are God's."

- 4. What can I do?

Philippians 4:13: "I can do all things through Christ which strengtheneth me."
Colossians 3:2: "Set your minds on things above, not on earthly things."
Mark 12:31: "Love your neighbor as you love yourself."

- 5. Where are you going?

Mark 16:15: "And He said unto them, go ye into all the world, and preach the Gospel to every creature."
2 Timothy 4:2: "Preach the word: be ready in season and out of season; reprove, rebuke, exhort; with great patience and instruction."

Questions to ask yourself

- Does my decision please God?
- Does my decision fit who I am?
- Does my decision consistent with the Bible?
- Does my decision give me peace?
- Does it build up the Kingdom of God?

You cannot change what you were born to do. Plus, you will not be satisfied until you do. Make a choice today to live out your purpose. It's not only for you but for others. You do know that, "You are saved to save others!" Come on, join me and let's get this work done before the return of the Lord!

EVANGELIST DORIS SMITH
KINGDOM LIFE COACH

Author Biography

I'm from a little town called Grenada, Mississippi. Yes, the crooked-letter and hump-back state. I have lived here most of my life. My Parents are both deceased, however; they still lives in my heart.

I am an Evangelist/Pastor; Author and a Kingdom Life Coach. I graduated from Grenada High School in 1980.

I got Born-again in 1996 and accepted my call in Ministry in 1997.

I graduated from Holmes Community College, Grenada, Mississippi in 2007 with an Associate in Elementary for Teaching/Crimminal Justice.

I have a Bachelor in Christian Psychology, in which I recieved in 2010. I have other Ministry Certificates from several other schools as well.

I am the Founder of Kingdom Ministry, which was started in July 2015. This Ministry is an Outreach Ministry. It consists of Jail Ministry, Nursing Home Ministry and a Clothing Ministry.

I have two (2) Beautiful daughters and a Son-in-Law. I also have five (5) grand-children. I actually have other children that calls me Ma' as well. I am a greatful/blessed Woman and OFTEN I'M SAYING, "THANK YOU GOD!"

Other Books Published
Facing Reality
A Conversation About the Good Old Days

INCLUDED QUOTES & REFERENCES FROM:
Mary T. Lathrap
Joyce Meyer
Facing Reality
Campbell Soup
Google Dictionary
Oxford Dictionary
New International Version Bible
King James Version Bible

Printed in the United States
by Baker & Taylor Publisher Services